Building
Christian Community

Catherine Martin

PILGRIMAGE

PAULIST PRESS
New York/Ramsey

ISBN: 0-8091-9311-6

Published by Paulist Press
545 Island Road
Ramsey, New Jersey 07446

Printed and bound in the United States of America

Contents

Foreword

"Then they recounted what had happened to them on the road and how they had come to recognize him in the breaking of the bread." (Lk 24:36)

To be human is to be on a journey. To be Christian is to believe we do not journey alone. The same Jesus who has gone on ahead to prepare a home for us has returned in his Spirit to accompany us all along the way.

Throughout our human pilgrimage we continue to meet him in the sharing of our lives and to recognize him clearly in the breaking of the bread.

PILGRIMAGE booklets are designed in response to an increasing demand for materials to be used by small Christian communities which are developing rapidly throughout the country. They emphasize five important elements necessary for strong community growth: mutual *support* in faith life and daily concerns; *sharing* of thoughts and spiritual insights rooted in Scripture; *prayer,* both personal and communal; *sound teaching* of Catholic faith; and *outreach* in service to the larger parish and community. The materials of PILGRIMAGE booklets cover a wide range of topics in order to nourish spiritual growth, communal development, and a strong support base for a variety of ministries.

Introduction

Community is intended to help your sharing group come to a better understanding about yourselves and your relationships to others. You, the members of this group, are the key to where the sessions will lead as you go through them. Remember that you as a group are responsible for your growth and the form your community takes. It is up to you to use the materials in the ways that you decide will best meet your needs. A suggested format is given but it is meant to be flexible. Adapt it to the needs of your group. The questions for sharing are designed so that you can choose from among those presented. If you wish to discuss more questions than can be handled in one session, reserve some for the next meeting. The purpose is to grow as a community, not to complete a set of sessions or activities. Trust that the Holy Spirit is in your midst and will guide you in your community development. Your love for one another will move you to pray and reflect together, to learn and serve together. Then you will go forward in confidence and peace together.

Suggestions for Leader

Your job is an important one — but not a demanding one.

Prayer

Developing a personal relationship with the Lord will help you to relate to the group. Your reflections on Scripture and spiritual writings will enrich your interpersonal relationships.

Preparation

Call to welcome each member of the group several days before the first meeting. Drop off the materials at the home so members can prepare for the meeting. The leader should be familiar with the materials suggested for each session.

Time

Each session should begin and end according to the schedule decided by the group.

Atmosphere

Create a relaxed atmosphere. Be respectful and supportive of each member. Encourage the expression of ideas and feelings. Avoid forcing your own viewpoint.

Format

Follow the suggested format but allow for flexibility to satisfy the needs of the group.

Scripture

A Bible should be available for each gathering. The person who proclaims the Word should have time to prepare the reading.

Sharing

Avoid the temptation to teach, lecture, or dominate the sharing. Encourage all members to participate but never pressure anyone. If the group strays from the topic, gently draw them back. If the sharing is fruitful, do not rush. It is not necessary to give responses to all the questions. Conflict and differences of opinion can bring about growth in a group, but must be handled with prudence.

Communication

Good communication skills are essential for group sharings. Members should be encouraged to be attentive listeners.

Confidentiality

Remind the group of the obligation to keep all sharings confidential.

Sharing Prayer

Praying spontaneously may be a new experience for many people. Members should have the freedom to pray aloud or remain silent. Be comfortable with short periods of silence.

Refreshments

Coffee, tea, and simple refreshments should be reserved until the end of the session.

Suggested Format

A. Opening Prayer: (5 min.)

Begin with a few moments to remind yourselves of the presence of God. Relax from your household and business concerns, leaving them in the hands of the Lord and direct your attention to the topic of reflection in your sharing group.

B. Reflection: (10 min.)

Read the reflection prior to each meeting. During the meeting re-read the reflection and the Scripture readings that are indicated.

C. Sharing: (35 min.)

Discuss those questions to which you wish to respond and/or include other questions which relate to the topic. At times you may wish to continue this discussion for more than one session. Feel free to do so.

D. Prayer: (20 min.)

Use the suggestions given or develop your own prayer service.

E. Faith in Action: (15 min.)

Be faithful to the process suggested, but add to it if you wish.

F. Assignment: (5 min.)

Review the Faith in Action assignment before leaving.

G. Our Father:

Join hands and pray the Our Father.

We Are Called to Live Community Life

Opening Prayer

See suggested format.

Spend a few minutes going around the circle having each person introduce himself or herself if necessary and offer some of the reasons why he or she has come to this group.

Reflection

The Father, the Son, and the Holy Spirit are a community of love. These three persons have always been together and share everything with one another — every thing they know, every desire they have, and every power they possess. The Father, the Son, and the Holy Spirit are so completely one with each other that any relationship with one of these persons is at once a relationship with the other two. God lives a community life.

The idea that God is three persons living and loving together is not something we can understand by ourselves. The Trinity is a mystery, which means it is a reality which our minds can never know completely. There is always something more we can learn about such a mystery. There are several Scripture passages in which Jesus tells us about the total unity of the Father, the Son, and the Holy Spirit. *Read John 14:6-10* and *John 14:23-26*.

The love that the persons of the Holy Trinity have does not keep them closed in upon themselves. The creation stories of Genesis tell us of God's choice to make a God-like being. "God created man/woman in his image; in the divine image he created him/her; male and female he created them." *(Genesis 1:27)*. God, from this beginning of human history created human persons to be in relationship with one another, to form community. From the start of our existence, therefore, there has been a deep inner urge for individuals to come together and care for one another. Undeniably the search for community often fails and a great temptation to withdrawal and isolation overcomes human beings from time to time, but the call to community is never completely suppressed. The creation story reminds us that we will never be completely human unless we strive to fulfill our calling to form a community of love.

Besides our relationships with other men and women, God has invited us to enter into an on-going relationship with him, both personally and as a community. Even beyond this marvelous reality is the realization that the type of relationship God wishes to have with individuals and with his people is not one of the ruler toward the ruled, but an interpersonal relationship of great love. Through the prophet Isaiah, God reveals the intensity of his love for us even when we do not seem to experience it. "Zion said, 'The Lord has forsaken me; my Lord has forgotten me.' Can a mother forget her infant, be without tenderness for the child of her womb? Even should she forget, I will never forget you. See, upon the palms of my hands I have written your name." *(Isaiah 49:14-16).*

God's life and ours are bound together. With personal concern God loves us as unique individuals. God loves our whole community who together form one people, one body. Our life in God is tied up with our life with one another. There is, therefore, a need for each one of us to strike a balance between the energies we put into our personal relationship with God and the energies we put into our relationships within the human community. The two cannot be separated. Moses, servant of God and the Hebrew people, gives us a model of the internalizing of solitude and community. *Read Exodus 33:11-17* to see an example of how God directed Moses during their time of intimate communication to provide for the needs of the total community.

Jesus, of course, gives us the definitive requirements for living our life to its full potential when he summarizes our human vocation as a call to love. "You shall love the Lord your God with your whole heart, with your whole soul, and with all your mind...you shall love your neighbor as yourself." *(Matthew 22:37-39)*

Sharing

(This section is designed so that you can choose from among the following questions. Your responses do not have to be completed in one session; you can continue your discussion for as many meetings as you wish. The purpose is to grow as a community not to complete a given number of sessions or activities.)

• What can the community life of the Trinity teach us?

- How will personal growth affect my participation in this community?
- What responsibilities do we have to each other in forming this small Christian community?
- How responsible do we feel for the building of God's kingdom here on earth?

Prayer

(Each week a different person could be responsible for preparing the prayer service, using the outline given or making up one for the group. Preparation includes gathering the special materials which will be needed.)

Play the song, *Though the Mountains May Fall* (from the album/cassette *Earthen Vessels* by the St. Louis Jesuits).

Leader: Say a prayer which includes thanking God for calling us to live a community life.

Silence or Shared Prayer — 5 minutes or more.

Starting with the Leader — one at a time — turn to the person on your right, take his/her hand, and say, "We are children of the same Father." Do this around the circle until all hands are joined.

Glory be...

Faith in Action

This portion of each meeting is essential. As Christians we can never limit our discussion to simply personal or interior concerns. We are asked to continue the mission of Jesus in making God's love real and visible in our world today.

Read James 2:14-26 for a summary of the connection between faith and action.

The *Faith in Action* part of each session is meant to lead this community to search out the needs around us today, to find out how these needs can be met, and then as individuals and as a group to respond. We are called to build the kingdom of God, a kingdom of love, of peace, of justice.

Each session will conclude with an assignment to promote faith in action. Fidelity to this assignment will be very important to the growth of the sharing group as a Christian community.

Assignment

Faith in Action

Before the next session list particular needs of people which can be addressed or situations which call for change.

Our Father: See suggested format.

Jesus Gathered a Community Together

Opening Prayer

See suggested format.

Reflection

When God, in his great love for us, decided to reveal himself as a human being, he did not manifest himself as an isolated, independent Savior. No, Emmanuel, God with us, Jesus, was born as a helpless, dependent baby — a member of a family. Jesus lived in this small community of love for many years. In beginning his active ministry Jesus chose to become part of a community. He sought a band of twelve with whom he spent most of his time, and then he gathered a group of disciples around the intimate group of apostles.

In looking at the people with whom Jesus related, we see that there were different levels of intimacy at which he related as a human being. He devoted much time, and even shared a common purse with the apostles and it was clearly recognized by those who knew Jesus at the time that these twelve chosen ones were his special followers. This did not close out, however, many others from staying close to him. We see that Jesus knew personally many people, for example, the seventy-two disciples, the group of women who devoted themselves to his physical care, and special friends like Martha, Mary, and Lazarus, who were so close to his heart that Jesus wept at the thought of Lazarus' death. Also, Jesus was constantly aware of, and sensitive to, all the other people with whom he came in contact. He took the initiative to heal the son of the widow of Naim, he knew when the hemorrhaging woman touched him, he undertook a lengthy conversation with the Samaritan woman at the well. In addition, Jesus participated in many community gatherings such as the wedding feast of Cana, meals with public sinners as well as with respective Pharisees, and synagogue services.

Jesus is the model of integrating human relationships with relationship with God. Before calling his apostles, Jesus spent time alone in the desert. When the disciples returned from spreading the good news to many towns, Jesus prayed aloud in praise of the Father, and he prayed with great intensity before his arrest. In all these examples we can realize that Jesus did not separate his prayer life from his interpersonal relationships. To see one example of how Jesus brought those he loved into his conversation with God, *read John 17:1-26*. To see how willing Jesus was to leave his solitude for the sake of others *read Mark 6:30-34*.

Each of us belongs to a variety of communities. We have many relationships with other people, each of which has its own level of intimacy. We relate differently to family members than to close friends, co-workers, co-parishioners, casual acquaintances. We are called to bring true love to each of these relationships, but the expressions of that love will be unique to each situation. Right here in this sharing group we have begun to form a community of love. Gradually we will explore what this community can mean for us and how we can best relate to one another in this group. Our call to love will lead us to seek a healthy balance between all our various relationships.

Living a fully human life as Jesus did, also means striking the balance in our individual lives between solitude and community. We need to bring all our relationships to prayer and be aware of God as he acts in the midst of our human communities. Like Jesus we must be flexible and seek extra prayer times in periods of special need, but never be so rigid that we cannot move from our quiet time to be with others who might need us just when we have decided to go apart for a while.

Sharing

(You may wish to extend your discussion for more than one session. Delete or add questions as the group decides.)

What qualities of Jesus' life with his apostles can we imitate?

How can our involvement in this group enrich our personal relationships?

Who are the people to whom we can minister or what situation are we called to change?

Prayer

Begin with the *Prayer Leader* saying aloud a prayer that he or she has written down or wishes to say spontaneously.

Play the song, *If God Is for Us* (from the album/cassette *Earthen Vessels* by the St. Louis Jesuits).

Silent Prayer — 5 minutes or more

Petitions

Leader: In thanksgiving for the example Jesus has given us of how to live in community, let us pray...

All: Lord, hear our prayer.

Leader: For the grace to be able to know the best way to integrate our relationship with God with our relationships with other people, let us pray...

All: Lord, hear our prayer.

Leader: That each of us may be a source of peace in all the communities to which we belong, let us pray...

All: Lord, hear our prayer.

Leader: That this sharing group may be faithful to our calling to be a community of love, let us pray...

All: Lord, hear our prayer.

Any member may now add a petition.
All respond to each petition: Lord, hear our prayer.
Then pray together: *The Prayer of St. Francis*

Lord, make me an instrument of your peace;
  where there is hatred, let me sow love;
  where there is injury, pardon;
  where there is doubt, faith;
  where there is despair, hope;
  where there is darkness, light;
and where there is sadness, joy.

Grant that I may not so much seek
  to be consoled, as to console;
  to be understood, as to understand;
  to be loved, as to love;
  for it is in giving, that we receive;
  it is in pardoning, that we are pardoned;
and it is in dying that we are born to eternal life.

Faith in Action

Share with one another the people in need or situations that need to be changed which you have observed since the last session. Have someone in the group write down each item. Gather as many needs as you can on your list.

Read the following list and add any which the group experiences as real needs which have not been listed.

Local high school or grade school improvement
Someone to shop for elderly people
Food for people who are hungry
Hospital visitors or people to visit homes for the aged
Relief for those in a crisis situation, fire, flood, earthquake

Better working conditions
Support for families
Help for troubled young people
More Christian values in government
Better television programming
Child care services for working parents
More spiritual growth opportunities for parishioners
Improved relations between Catholics and other churches.

When the group's list is complete, read it aloud to the whole group. Each person should choose one or two iems on the list to think about further. Make sure that those responsible for each need have written them down.

Assignment
Faith in Action
During the time between sessions, each person should talk to at least two other people regarding the needs they have on their list. Write down the ways you think the needs could be met.
Our Father. See suggested format.

Jesus Set Up a
Continuing Community

Opening Prayer

See suggested format.

Reflection

Jesus prepared his followers to share in his mission of proclaiming the coming of God's kingdom. Jesus commissioned them to continue spreading the Good News. In the final hours he was to spend with them Jesus prayed, "I do not pray for them alone. I pray also for those who will believe in me through their word, that all may be one as you, Father, are in me, and I in you." *(John 17:20-21)*

Jesus did not call each apostle aside and give each one a separate task, but rather spoke to the whole group. Jesus set aside this band of people to be a continuing community. He gave a common mission to them to draw all people into the oneness they shared in Christ. This common vocation coupled with the command to love one another were the charter of the Church Jesus initiated and sustains.

It took the apostles a little while to realize the implications of their new role and in the beginning they stayed together out of sheer fright. But, true to his promise, Jesus sent his Spirit upon those gathered in the upper room on Pentecost, and they began to "make bold proclamations as the Spirit prompted them." *(Acts 2:4)*

Throughout the writings of the young Church, we find references to the communitarian nature of the call to follow Jesus.

"The body is one and has many members, but all the members, many though they are, are one body; and so it is with Christ...you then, are the body of Christ. Every one of you is a member of it." *(1 Corinthians 12:12,27)*

"...You are strangers and aliens no longer. No, you are fellow citizens of the saints and members of the household of God. You form a building which rises on the foundation of the apostles and prophets, with Christ Jesus himself as the capstone. Through him the whole structure is fitted together and takes shape as a holy temple in the Lord; in him you are being built into this temple; to become a dwelling place for God in the Spirit.-- *(Ephesians 2:19-22)* "You, however, are a 'chosen race, a royal priesthood, a holy nation, a people he claims for his own to proclaim the glorious works of the One who called you from darkness into his marvelous light. Once you were no people, but now you are God's people...*(1 Peter 2:9-10).*

The early Church, the Church as it has existed throughout the years, and the Church of today are still the same people of God called to be a loving community. We are historically one unit and we are also geographically one global community. We are one body with the people of our parish, with the local churches of our own country, with the Church of Africa, Latin America, and every church throughout the world. In different ages of history we acted out our common faith in Jesus in ways very different than we do today. In different countries we live out our commitment today in varied forms, but we are still one body, with each member of the body fulfilling a unique role for the good of all. We all have that shared mission from God to spread his kingdom and we all live under the one commandment to love. *Read Hebrews 13:1-8* to hear an exhortation given to the Church that believes Jesus and his message transcend time and place.

Sharing

(This is your community. You choose the questions to which you will respond at this meeting. Some questions might be reserved for your next session.)

- How is our mission a continuation of the work of the apostles?
- How can we share the Good News in our parish?
- What can we do to enrich our understanding of the history of the Church?
- How could we be influential in providing opportunities for our parishioners to enrich their understanding of Church.

Prayer:

Light a candle and place it in the center of the group.
Turn off the lights.

Leader:
Let us take a few moments to pray about our connection to all other members of Christ's body throughout time. Each of

16

us is asked to think of one historical figure whom we know from Scripture, or from the lives of saints, or one of the holy people who has lived during our lifetime. Spend some time thinking about that person's life and asking him or her to guide you in loving a good Christian life.

(Five minutes of silence)

Now each of us is asked to think of a country other than our own and of the people who live there. Spend some time asking Jesus to help you realize more fully that you are linked to all Christians throughout the world in a special way. Ask for the grace to work in union with your brothers and sisters around the world who have the same Father as you have.

(Five minutes of silence)

Play the song, *Be Not Afraid* (from the album/cassette *Earthen Vessels* by the St. Louis Jesuits).

Faith in Action

Share with one another the ways you have discovered to meet each of the needs on your list. Have someone responsible for writing down the ways that are mentioned.

As you hear the ideas expressed it should become evident that there are many ways to approach any one problem. For the sake of some order you will now be asked to divide your solutions into two categories, direct service or root change. *Direct Service* should include every solution which helps take care of an immediate need with an immediate form of assistance. *Root Change* should include every solution which goes to the source of a problem and works toward prevention or changes the way the problem is handled at a higher level. Take for example the need for an improved situation in the local grade school. Direct Service could include volunteering to be a lunch supervisor so that there are less disruptive meal times. Root Change could include becoming active in the Parent-Teachers Association and helping formulate the policy on discipline. This need requires both types of solutions. Any person or group can work at both direct service and root change in areas about which they are concerned.

Have someone read the solutions; as a group decide which ones are direct services and which ones are root changes. For example, collecting food for the hungry is a direct service, and writing to a congressperson to support legislation to increase our food commitments to poor countries is a root change.

Assignment

Faith in Action

Before the next session, each person is to call or visit one organization that deals with the areas of concern he or she selected at the last session. Get as much information as you can about what services are provided by this group. Include both direct service and root change solutions that the organization is providing. The Social Concerns Committee of your parish might be able to provide information for you.

Our Father. See suggested format.

The First Christians: Faithful to the Teachings of the Apostles

Opening Prayer

See suggested format.

Reflection

Immediately after the account of Pentecost the Acts of the Apostles gives a beautiful summary of the communal life of the early Church. This paragraph will be the main source of reflection for the next four sessions in particular.
(Read Acts 2:42-47)

Four elements of community are listed in the first verse of this passage, i.e., the apostles' instruction, communal life, breaking of bread, and prayers. Let us begin our reflection of the life of the first Christians by looking more closely at this community's devotion to the teaching of the apostles.

From the earliest gatherings of the disciples of Jesus after his death and resurrection, the apostles were acknowledged as the leaders of the community. Before Pentecost, Peter stood up in the midst of about one hundred twenty disciples and called for a replacement for Judas among the twelve. One criterion used was that the new member would have to have been one of the company of believers while Jesus moved among them "from the baptism of John until the day he was taken up." *(Acts 1:22)* The other criterion was God's free choice and so after selecting two potential candidates the community prayed, "Lord you can read everyone's heart; show us therefore which of these two you have chosen to take over this ministry and apostolate..." *(Acts 1:24-25)*

Personal relationship with Jesus over a long period of time and the Lord's own call were recognized by the assembly as signs of leadership. The letters of the apostles to the local communities of the church attest to the fact that the twelve continued to guide the members as they searched to understand the message of Jesus better and to find the best ways of living out their lives in fidelity to that message.

It was not an easy road to discover the fitting guidelines for putting the kingdom of God into visible form in that particular age and that same challenge has always remained. The public disagreements between Peter and Paul show clearly that no perfect plan of action was hand delivered to the apostles for implementation. *Read Galatians 2:1-14* to see a combination of spiritual ways of relating to leadership.

Putting the Gospel into practice was and is a growing process; constantly being refined, adapted to new circumstances, and shaped to respond to new needs. Structures grew up gradually and have been changed to meet new challenges. God still continues to lead us through human beings of his own choice. We are called to pray for good leaders, to recognize their authority, listen to their teachings, place our concerns before them, and admonish them when they do not act in conformity with the Gospel message they proclaim.

Fidelity to the teaching of the apostles was essential for the early Christian community and it is essential for the Christian community of today. There are different functions in the community and we need to recognize that reality, seek to discern our own gifts, and relate in harmony with all the other members according to their roles. Urging us to live in perfect unity, St. Paul speaks of the calling we have received from Jesus, and then writes, "It is he who gave apostles, prophets, evangelists, pastors, and teachers in roles of service for the faithful to build up the body of Christ, till we become one in faith and in the knowledge of God's Son, and form that perfect man who is Christ come to full stature. Let us then be children no longer, tossed here and there, carried about by every wind of doctrine that originates in human trickery and skill in proposing error. Rather let us profess the truth in love and grow to the full maturity of Christ the head. Through him the whole body grows, and with the proper functioning of the new members joined firmly together by each supporting ligament, builds itself up in love" *(Ephesians 4:11-16)*.

Sharing

(Remember: share your responses at your own pace.)
- How are we as a community providing leadership for our local Church?
- How are our lives proclaiming our belief in the Lord Jesus?
- What could we as a community do to verbalize our Christian belief system...in our parish...in our city...in our nation?
- What more can we be doing to bring about change for the oppressed?

Prayer

(Take turns reading these sections slowly. You will be praying the Eucharistic Prayer I, that prayer which the Church uses at the Liturgy. Unite your heart and mind to believers throughout the world who are celebrating the Liturgy now.)

1st Person:
We come to you, Father, with praise and thanksgiving through Jesus Christ your Son. Through him we ask you to accept and bless our lives, the gifts we offer you in sacrifice.

2nd Person:
We offer them for your holy Catholic Church, watch over it, Lord, and guide it; grant it peace and unity throughout the world. We offer them for our Pope_____, for Archbishop_____, for all our bishops, and for all who hold and teach the Catholic faith that comes to us from the apostles.

3rd Person:
Remember, Lord, your people, especially those for whom we now pray — *(pause,* go around the circle with each person saying aloud the name of a person for whom he or she would like the group to pray). Remember all of us gathered here before you. You know how firmly we believe in you and dedicate ourselves to you. We offer you this sacrifice of praise for ourselves and those who are dear to us. We pray to you, our living and true God, for our well-being and redemption.

4th Person:
In union with the whole church we honor Mary, the ever-virgin mother of Jesus Christ our Lord and God. We honor Joseph, her husband, the apostles and martyrs Peter and Paul, Andrew, James, John, Thomas, James, Philip, Bartholomew, Matthew, Simon and Jude; we honor Linus, Cletus, Clement, Sixtus, Cornelius, Cyprian, Lawrence, Chrysogonus, John and Paul, Cosmas and Damian, and all the saints. May their merits and prayers gain us your constant help and protection.

5th Person:
Remember, Lord, those who have died and have gone before us marked with the sign of faith, especially those for whom we now pray *(pause* — go around the circle with each person naming aloud one deceased person for whom he or she would like the group to pray). May these and all who sleep in Christ, find in your presence light, happiness, and peace.

6th Person:

For ourselves, too, we ask some share in the community of your apostles and martyrs, with John the Baptist, Stephen, Matthias, Barnabas, Ignatius, Alexander, Marcellinus, Peter, Felicity, Perpetua, Agatha, Lucy, Agnes, Cecilia, Anastasia, and all the saints.

Though we are sinners, we trust in your mercy and love.

Do not consider what we truly deserve, but grant us your forgiveness.

Through Christ our Lord you give us all these gifts. You fill them with life and goodness, you bless them and make them holy.

All:

Through him, with him, in him, in the unity of the Holy Spirit, all glory and honor is yours, almighty Father, for ever and ever. Amen.

Faith in Action

Share the information you gathered on organizations which present some solutions to the needs around you. Distribute any pamphlets or written literature you were able to obtain.

Assignment

Faith in Action

Share the information you gathered about the organizations with three family members and/or friends.

The group leader should invite a member of the Parish Council to speak to the group at the next session about how the Parish Council sees the needs of the local community, and what its plans are to help meet these needs. Perhaps the chairperson of the Social Concerns Committee would be a good representative to invite.

Our Father: See suggested format.

The First Christians: Faithful to Community Life

Opening Prayer

See suggested format.

Reflection

After saying that the first believers devoted themselves to communal life, the author of Acts goes on to say, "Those who believed shared all things in common; they would sell their property and goods, dividing everything on the basis of each one's needs." *(Acts 2:44-45)* The early Christians lived an intense common life. This description can be overwhelming to us and we may want to explain it away. Not every early believer followed this pattern and not all are called to do so today; however, this image of communal life still remains as a great witness, a haunting reminder that following Jesus can change a person's (our) whole value system and life style.

One thing stands out clearly, the Christian concept of community and love for one another must be expressed in action. The concern for the physical needs of all members is as important as moral or spiritual support of one another. A Christian cannot love a person without caring for the whole person. St. John is well known for giving strong testament to this statement, "I ask you, how can God's love survive in a man (woman) who has enough of this world's goods, yet closes his (her) heart to his (her) brother (sister) when he (she) sees him (her) in need. Little children, let us love in deed and in truth and not merely talk about it" *(1 John 3:17-18)*.

The extent to which caring for the physical needs of all members was practiced led to a major change in the life of the Christian community. The community selected several members and appointed them to do this work. *Read Acts 6:1-6* to see the very human complaints which were the basis for this new ministry.

It is clear that the first community was a living body responding to needs with new structures and open to challenges whenever they presented themselves. Certain elements of the community did remain the same, however, and these were the qualities which gave evidence that they were followers of Jesus, and that they loved one another. These qualities are the same gifts of grace that we as a church have received from the Holy Spirit. There was, and continues to be, a need for reminders and encouragement for the community to nurture these gifts and live them to their full potential. The epistles are filled with such exhortations and give us some idea of the variety of ways in which Christian love can be expressed. *Read* the following passages for some of the expectations held for the Christian community. *Philippians 2:1-7, Colossians 3:12-17, 1 Peter 1:13-17.*

Though part of a community we retain our individuality, developing to our full potential in every way possible. The good of the community depends upon each person's uniqueness and giftedness. No individual has everything; together the members make a meaningful, useful body. We must become fully ourselves and then put our full selves at the service of the total community, fitting together as one. "There are different gifts, but the same spirit; there are different ministries, but the same Lord; there are different works, but the same God who accomplishes all of them in everyone. To each person the manifestation of the Spirit is given for the common good." *(1 Corinthians 12:4-7) Read 1 Corinthians 12:12-26* to see the importance of our differences and our need to work together.

Sharing

(Remember: share your responses at your own pace.)
- What gifts do each of us possess which are meant to be used in this community?
- What can each of us do to help the other become fully human?
- What immediate action can we take to alter an unjust situation affecting the poor, handicapped, elderly?

Prayer

Leader:

God, come to my assistance. Glory be to the Father and to the Son and to the Holy Spirit, as it was in the beginning is now and ever shall be, world without end. Amen.

Wherever you are, Lord, there is mercy, there is truth.

Reader 1:

Psalm 89:1-18

Leader:
When the Son of God came into this world, he was born of David's line.

Reader 2:
Psalm 89:19-29

Leader:
Once for all I swore to my servant David: his dynasty shall never fail.

Reader 3:
Psalm 80:30-37

Leader:
When we listen to your word, our minds are filled with light.

All:
It is the lowly heart that understands.

Reader 4:
I John 4:11-21

Silent Reflection — Five minutes or more

Reader 5:
Let the person truly possessed by the love of Christ keep his commandment. Who can express the binding power of divine love? Who can find words for the splendor of its beauty? Beyond all description are the heights to which it lifts us. Love unites us to God; it *cancels innumerable sins,* has no limits to its endurance, bears everything patiently. Love is neither servile nor arrogant. It does not provoke schisms or form cliques, but always acts in harmony with others. By it all God's chosen ones have been sanctified; without it, it is impossible to please him. Out of love the Lord took us to himself; because he loved us and it was God's will, our Lord Jesus Christ gave his life's blood for us — he gave his body for our body, his soul for our soul.

See then, beloved, what a great and wonderful thing love is, and how inexpressible its perfection. Who are worthy to possess it unless God makes them so? To him therefore, we must turn, begging of his mercy that there may be found in us a love free from human partiality and beyond reproach.

Happy are we, beloved, if love enables us to live in harmony and in the observance of God's commandments, for then it will also gain for us the remission of our sins. Scripture pronounces happy those whose transgressions are pardoned, whose sins are forgiven. *Happy the one,* it says, *to whom the Lord imputes no fault, on whose lips there is no guile.* This is the blessing given those whom God has chosen through Jesus Christ our Lord. To him be glory forever and ever. Amen.

(From a letter to the Corinthians by Saint Clement I, Pope Christian Prayer: the Liturgy of the Hours)
Leader:
Father, let the gift of your life continue to grow in us, drawing us from death to faith, hope, and love. Keep us alive in Christ Jesus. Keep us watchful in prayer and true to his teachings till your glory is revealed in us. Grant this through Christ our Lord.
All:
Amen.
(A loaf of unsliced bread and a bottle of wine will be needed for the prayer service next week.)

Faith in Action

Have the leader introduce the representative from the Parish Council who will speak on the needs of the local community and the plans to help meet those needs.

After the presentation, members of the group should ask questions they may have. Be sure to invite your guest for coffee and casual conversation after the meeting.

Assignment

Faith in Action
Choose one need which has surfaced and do one concrete action to help take care of that need.
Our Father:
See suggested format.

The First Christians: Faithful to the Breaking of the Bread

Opening Prayer

See suggested format.

Reflection

For persons who like to be together mealtime is meaningful. People nourish one another's spirits and deepen their love for each other when sharing at special meals. Jesus knew and blessed the mixture of natural and spiritual nourishment that takes place at mealtimes. He is often depicted in the Gospels as sharing supper with other people. The most significant meal he shared was his final one with the apostles. Within the context of the meal, Jesus shared the message that he would remain as our nourishment.

The early Christians celebrated the presence of Jesus during meals shared in their homes. This was the initial form of celebrating the Liturgy. The portion of the meal in which the early Christians re-enacted the transformation of bread and wine into the body and blood of Jesus became known as the breaking of the bread. As it is depicted in *Acts 2:46* "...in their homes they broke bread. With exultant and sincere hearts they took their meals in common."

We continue to celebrate the real presence of Jesus in our midst. The Christian community still gathers to eat of the bread and drink from the cup which have become the body and blood of Jesus. The Eucharist remains the source and center of our community celebration, a celebration of the love Jesus has for us and the love we are called to give one another. Jesus is the source and center of the community. In addition to his sacramental presence, Jesus is uniquely present in each person as we gather in love to be his body.

St. Paul says of the Eucharist, "Is not the cup of blessing we bless a sharing in the blood of Christ? And is not the bread we break a sharing in the body of Christ? Because the loaf of bread is one, we, many though we are, are one body, for we all partake of the one loaf." *(I Corinthians 10:16-17).*

Vatican Council II took up the topic of the Eucharist and its call to community and service in several of its documents. Here is one example, "No Christian community, however, can be built up unless it has its basis and center in the celebration of the most Holy Eucharist. Here, therefore, all education in the spirit of community must originate. If this celebration is to be sincere and thorough, it must lead to various works of charity and mutual help, as well as to missionary activity and to different forms of Christian witness." *(The Ministry of Priests,* Decree on the Ministry and Life of Priests. The Documents of Vatican II)

The early Christian community was faithful to the breaking of the bread in both the reception of Jesus in the sacramental signs of bread and wine and in the giving of Jesus to one another through the sign of real love. We, too, need to be faithful to the breaking of the bread and to allow Jesus to transform our lives into signs of his presence.

Sharing

(Choose the questions to which you will respond during this session.)

• What can we do to enrich the celebration of the Eucharistic Liturgy in our parish?
• How have the people whom we served made us aware of the presence and love of Jesus?
• How can we help each other to be more aware of the presence and love of Jesus in our lives?

Prayer

Play the song, *The Lord Jesus* (from the album/cassette *Listen* by the Weston Priory)
Reader 1:
    Mark 14:22-26
Reader 2:
    John 13:2-15
Silent Reflection — 3 to 5 minutes

Response

Leader:
    For the times we have not been grateful for the special presence of Jesus in the Eucharist,
All:
    Lord, have mercy.

Leader:

For the times when we have not recognized that the people around us are the Body of Christ,

All:

Christ, have mercy.

Leader:

For the times we have not shared our lives in service, as Jesus has shared himself with us in the Eucharist,

All:

Lord, have mercy.

(The prayer will be continued after *Faith in Action)*

Faith in Action

Report on the measure you took to help solve a need. How did you feel about doing it?

Assignment

Faith in Action

If the need on which you are working requires additional response, continue on your project. If you have completed your work, choose a different need. Once again perform a concrete action to help a person or to change a situation.

Continuation of Prayer Service:

Leader:

Sharing bread and wine with friends is a warm, friendly gesture. It is not only a part of our religious tradition, but it is also an expression of health, peace, and love.

Jesus took bread and wine, these natural elements of a celebration and gave them new meaning. He made them signs of his life with us.

So let us celebrate by sharing bread and wine. As we break bread together, let us remember that we share more than food. We are sharing our laughter, our joy, our cares and concerns, ourselves. "The fact that there is only one loaf means that, though there are many of us, we form a single body because we all have a share in this one loaf." *(I Corinthians 10:17)*

All:

Our Father...

Share the bread and wine now...Enjoy!

The First Christians: Faithful to Prayer

Opening Prayer

See suggested format.

Reflection

Prayer was a constant reality in the life of the early Christians. They knew God was close at hand and was lovingly involved in their lives. They praised, thanked, asked for forgiveness, interceded with God, and listened for his response. Relationships were rooted in a relationship to a loving Father, a personal Spirit who enlivened them, and Jesus who had been raised and was living in their midst.

Scripture records the prayer habits of the early Christian community. "They went to the temple area together every day, while in their homes they broke bread. With exultant and sincere hearts they took their meals in common, praising God..." *(Acts 2:46-47)* The first Christians continued to pray in the temple together according to their Jewish tradition and then they carried their prayer into the midst of joyful community meals. Communal, as well as personal prayer, was a very important part of their life.

The Christian heritage of prayer finds its roots in the accounts of the intimate relationships between God and his chosen people. *Read Exodus 33:12-17* to see how Moses conversed with God. The expressive song prayers or Psalms of David have been an unfailing source of inspiration for people throughout the ages.

For Christians Jesus is the pre-eminent model of a prayerful person. We read of his going apart to pray as well as praying aloud while among his disciples. He speaks in praise and thanks and petition. He asks for his own needs and the needs of his friends and the needs of all people. Jesus prays for us, too. For some examples of Jesus at prayer read *Matthew 11:25-27, Mark 2:35, Mark 6:41, Luke 5:16, Luke 22:39-46* and *John 17*.

Scripture provides us with accounts of Jesus encouraging his followers to enter into personal communion with God in prayer.

"Again I tell you, if two of you join your voices on earth to pray for anything whatever, it shall be granted you by my Father in heaven." *(Matthew 18:19)*
"In your prayer do not rattle on like the pagans. They think they will win a hearing by the sheer multiplication of words. Do not imitate them. Your Father knows what you need before you ask him." *(Matthew 6:7-8).*
"My command to you is: Love your enemies, pray for your persecutors." *(Matthew 5:44)*

These are just a few examples of Jesus' words on prayer. The writers of the epistles inserted numerous passages about prayer in their letters to the Christian communities. The church throughout the ages has remained a praying community comprised of many prayerful individuals.

There are certain aspects about prayer that seem mysterious. We enter into a relationship with a hidden yet intimate God. Prayer touches our bodies as well as our souls and affects the way we live. Prayer is unique to each person and has its own expression for each community of people. We can never know all there is to know of prayer or experience all there is to experience in prayer. We enter into prayer in faith, believing that God has called us to be in communion with him. We trust that he will lead us according to his own design into a deep awareness of the loving ways in which he wishes to relate to us. Our task is to remain faithful to prayer and God will fill up our weakness. "The Spirit, too, helps us in our weakness, for we do not know how to pray as we ought; but the Spirit himself makes intercession for us with groanings that cannot be expressed in speech. He who searches hearts knows what the Spirit means, for the Spirit intercedes for the saints as God himself wills." *(Romans 8:26-27).*

Sharing

(Remember: Share your responses at your own pace.)
- How can we enrich our prayer life in this community?
- How can we enrich the prayer life of our parish?
- What can I do to strengthen my personal prayer?
- Prayer in my family?
- What can I do to strengthen prayer in my family?

Prayer

Light a candle and place in the center of the group. Turn off the lights in the room.

Play the song *Seek the Lord* (from the album/cassette *Earthen Vessels* by the St. Louis Jesuits)

Spend ten minutes in quiet prayer talking to the Lord in your own words and listening for his response.

All: Let us join hands and pray, Our Father...

Faith in Action

Each person should report what action he or she took between this and the last session to alleviate a need. Share your feelings regarding the action.

It may be clear at this point that direct service, helping someone in an immediate crisis, is more quickly accomplished than root change, working to change situations. Time, patience, love, and concern are needed for serving others.

Assignment

Faith in Action

As a group choose one direct service area which you will address before the next session.

Glory be...

Elements of Community

Opening Prayer

See suggested format.

Reflection

Each of us belongs to several communities. We belong to a family — a parish — a network of close friends — an office or work group — and to this sharing community. We must constantly be alert to keep a proper balance in our relationship to the people of each community to which we belong. We must make decisions at various times to determine our degree of involvement in each group. No one can make these decisions for anyone else.

Besides the personal responsibility to create a balance of our time and energy in various groups, we also have a responsibility to maintain a Christian atmosphere in each community to which we belong. This is particularly true of this sharing group which has deliberately gathered as a Christian community. We need to reflect on the elements of community expressed in Scripture and see how we can be faithful to our commitment to build a Christian community.

For this session then we will change our format somewhat. We will begin to take the time to look at our sharing group and talk about how we should be functioning as a Christian community. A series of Scripture passages and questions are given as a starting point for reflection, but they are not meant to be limiting. Any member can bring up additional points that may be pertinent to the group. Do not be ruled by time; it may take more than one meeting to complete this sharing. The purpose is to reflect on our experiences and decide how we can best incorporate the elements of Christian community into our gatherings.

Take some quiet time to reflect on the Scripture passages and questions before sharing your responses. Record any decisions that are made so that the group can refer to them at a later date.

- What has brought us together as a community?
- What is special about this group?
  On fidelity to the teachings of the apostles, the Church (Learning) *Read I John 1:1-4.*

- How can we make sure that we are faithful to the teachings of the apostles?
- How can we build in time for learning more about Scripture and church teaching through tapes, a speaker, on-going learning?

On fidelity to community — local and global (community and service) *Read John 13:1-17.*
- How can we be faithful to this community?
- How can we show real concern for one another?
- How can we integrate our experiences in this community with our family and the other communities of which we are a part?
- What can we do to help other parishioners form small communities?
- How do we keep from closing in on ourselves or becoming a clique?
- How are we serving the needs of others, locally and geographically distant?

On fidelity to the Eucharist *Read Luke 22:14-20*
- How can we be faithful to the Eucharist?
- What can we do to make the Eucharistic Liturgy a celebration for our parish family?

On fidelity to prayer (Prayer and Scripture) *Read Ephesians 3:12-21*
- How can we be faithful to prayer?
- What can we do to enrich our personal and communal prayer?

To conclude *Read Hebrews 6:7-12*

Prayer

Read *Romans 15:1-7*
Quiet Reflection
Leader:
Father, hear our petitions as we place before you our prayers for the needs of our community.

(Spontaneous prayers of petition)
Leader:
As we continue to search out God's will for our community, let us ask the Holy Spirit to guide us by singing, *Come Holy Ghost.*

Come Holy Ghost

Come Holy Ghost, Creator blest,
And in our hearts, take up your rest

Come with your grace, and heavenly aid.
To fill the hearts which you have made,
To fill the hearts which you have made.

O Comforter, to you we cry,
You heavenly gift of God most high,
You font of life, and fire of love,
And sweet anointing from above,
And sweet anointing from above.

Praise be to you, Father and Son,
And Holy Spirit with them one.
And may the Son on us bestow,
The gifts that from the Spirit flow,
The gifts that from the Spirit flow.

Faith in Action

Discuss the direct service action which you completed as a group. Share some of the ways in which the people you serve are touching your life.

Assignment

Faith in Action

As a group choose one area where there is a need for root change. Work on the solution, taking as much time as needed to bring about change. Remind each other that change often takes time.

Our Father: See suggested format.

Building Community

Opening Prayer

See suggested format.

Reflection

Members of a group must work hard to develop a community, constantly striving to improve their relationships.

A healthy community is always engaged in a growing process, learning more, deepening its relationship with God and among its members, finding new ways to reach out in love to others beyond the group.

Read Romans 12:9-21 for an exhortation on the proper functioning of a Christian community. We are reminded here of some of the attitudes that need to be developed — affection, respect, hospitality, prayerfulness, sympathy. Our behavior in community is rooted in our attitudes, both those inside each individual's heart, and those developed within the group through our interaction. The Christian community is a human community and we need to be aware of that to understand how we can become the kind of caring group we would like to be.

We must realize that each individual who belongs to the group is a combination of a unique history, a special personality, and the particular graces God has given to this individual. No one can fully understand another person; each of us has parts unknown to others. There is always something new that can be discovered. For other people to come to know a person more fully, the individual has to first reveal something of himself or herself. We know that each person is precious and lovable because God has created and loved each of us, but we know little else until we can share with one another.

Because of our individuality each of us relates to others in unique ways. A room full of individuals talking, listening, and being present to one another creates a special kind of inter-personal dynamic or interaction. This changes from group to group because of the different combinations of individuals. The interaction changes somewhat each time a new person joins the group. It is good sometimes to stop and reflect on how we relate to one another in this group. Certain people may talk more frequently than others. Some people may fidget when there is a lag in conversation. Some individuals will show appreciation each time someone shares an idea or a story.

When we are serious about working to build up our community there are certain resources we can use. The first are internal resources, i.e., reaching within ourselves and bringing forth those attitudes and actions which best reflect who we are. The second are spiritual resources, i.e., prayer and Scriptural reflections both as individuals and as a group. The third are external resources, i.e., inviting a person who is trained in group dynamics to observe the group. Also, members could glean insights from books and magazine articles on community building. The fourth and final resource is the most important one, but one which we do not control, i.e., the action of the Holy Spirit. We must always be confident that God is at work among us building up this community, and that through the Holy Spirit, he will bring to fulfillment the good work that has begun. *Read Ephesians 1:13-23.*

Sharing

- Talk about an area in your life which is being healed since you became a member of this community.
- How are you developing the gift that you identified at a previous session?
- What means have you discovered for personal growth that might be helpful to the other members of your community?

Prayer

Leader:
Father, you have given us many gifts within this community. You have blessed each one of us with special graces for the building up of your Church. We praise you and we thank you for these blessings and we ask you to help us use our gifts in love and service.

Light *one candle* and dim the room lights. The LEADER, while holding the candle, prays in thanksgiving for the special talents or personal traits of the person on his or her left, and then passes the candle to that person. Each person repeats this procedure until everyone in the group has had a chance to pray.

Play the song, *Praise the Lord, My Soul* (from the album/cassette *Earthen Vessels* by the St. Louis Jesuits.)

Faith in Action

Discuss the action which you had taken to bring about a root change. Surface any obstacles which hinder progress.

Assignment

Faith in Action

Formulate the direction you will take to bring about change in the situation you had selected. Pray to the Holy Spirit to let you know if there is another area of need which you as an individual or as part of a group should be working to solve. Spend five minutes each day praying about this matter.

Our Father: See suggested format.

Pitfalls of Community

Opening Prayer

See suggested format.

Reflection

Every relationship has its ups and downs. Community life is also subject to the rhythms of relationships among the members. The beauty we used to see in the unique qualities of individuals in the group may become annoying differences. Conflicts may arise which make the atmosphere during a meeting tense. Some members may gradually stop preparing for the meeting and will then sit passively at the gathering. How does all this happen in a group of dedicated people trying to live a Christian way of life? To some extent, it is because we are fragile earthen vessels, and to some extent it is because we are sinners.

First of all, we have limitations as individuals and as a group. We have emotional highs and lows, physically painful days, concerns which block our reasoning power. *Read 2 Corinthians 4:1-10* for an image of weakness as the means God uses to manifest his power. Some of our pressures come from within but we are also affected by outside pressures, such as family difficulties, work tensions, friends who require much of our energy, and time limits. Each of us acts differently, depending on how much pressure is on us at a given time. We need to recognize and accept that in ourselves, but we must be aware that these are forces affecting the lives of every other member in the group as well.

Sin is another factor in creating difficulties in a group. Jealousy, anger, pride, selfishness, and impatience may be expressed in the group. No individual is free from sin and therefore, at some time, each person is capable of disrupting the community. Many of the epistles are letters to communities that were being distressed by sin among the members.

Read Galatians 5:13-26 for one exhortation by Paul against sinful behavior in the community at Galatia.

When difficulties arise in community life the challenge is to work through the hard times. In the midst of problems we need more than ever to be aware of the presence of Jesus in our midst. He is our hope and our source of healing. We should not give up on ourselves or on the community. It is Jesus who has called us together, who loves us just as we are, and who will bring us to new life. *Read Romans 5:1-8* for a reassurance of our cause for hope.

We need each other in order to become whole. It is only within a community that we can accurately come to know our own gifts, feelings, strengths, and weaknesses. We reflect our image on others as in a shiny surface, so that we can better know who we are.

Growth as individuals and as a community means change. Each difficult moment in community has a hidden opportunity for growth. We must take the risk to search out that opportunity and seek the courage to use it for growth.

Sharing

- What have you experienced as some of the ups and downs in our sharing group?
- Where do you feel we are now?
- How have we grown as a community?
- How can we influence other parishioners to form small Christian communities?

Prayer

Play the song, *Earthen Vessels* (from the album/cassette *Earthen Vessels* by the St. Louis Jesuits).
Read:
   Luke 22:39-46
Quiet Reflection
Read:
   Matthew 25:1-13
Shared Prayer
Leader:
   Lord, keep us from temptation. We cannot resist alone. Your treasure is in earthen vessels. Help us to stay awake, to stay close to you, to be ready for all the circumstances we have yet to meet in your service. Lord, help us to be true to you and to this community of love.
Read:
   Psalm 32

Faith in Action

Share with one another the results of your reflection and prayer since the last session. What needs are closest to your heart? What needs do you feel you should be serving on a regular basis? What needs would you like the group to address on a regular basis?

Assignment
Faith in Action
  Select one of the needs and decide the plan of action.
Our Father: See suggested format.

Healing in Community

Opening Prayer

See suggested format.

Reflection

Forgiveness should be a hallmark of our community life. There is healing in forgiveness. It is a sign of the presence of God in our midst. *Read Luke 6:36-42* and *Matthew 18:21-35.* Not only should each of us be ready to forgive others, but we must also be ready to seek forgiveness from the community for our own healing. "Indeed, sorrow for God's sake produces a repentance without regrets, leading to salvation..." *(2 Corinthians 7:10).*

Healing in community requires an attitude of openness, a willingness to honestly look at ourselves, our community, and our relationships. Sometimes we are so deeply involved in the situation that we find it hard to step back and look at what is happening. Then, we should invite someone from the outside, perhaps a staff member, to help us work through a difficult time. For the most part, however, we should be able to deal with problem areas if we set up a regular schedule of evaluation or examination of life for our community. The process we set up will work if we are gentle and loving in handling problems and conflicts. This calls for trusting one another, believing that each person is seeking the good of the whole community.

An examination of life process should be set up by the community. It should be rooted in prayer, include open conversation about issues and attitudes, and lead to concrete decisions. A prayer service of forgiveness should conclude each evaluation session. This will help us to remember that we are not solely responsible for the success of our community venture. We are in God's hands. Our sharing group and its relationships should not be seen as a heavy burden, but as a support along the way. We cannot take ourselves too seriously. God is with us. As we work through problem areas we must be ready to move on, leaving the past behind, knowing we have honestly faced the situation.

Some of the signs of the Spirit against which we should measure the quality of our relationships are given in St. Paul's letter to the Galatians. "The fruit of the spirit is love, joy, peace, patient endurance, kindness, generosity, faith, gentleness, and self-control" *(Galatians 5:22)*. Where these qualities exist the Spirit of God is present and active in a community. Another way to evaluate ourselves is to examine our fidelity to the essentials of community life, learning, sharing, outreach, prayer, and mutual support.

Sharing

Here is an outline of a sample evaluation session. Read it carefully.

I. Prayer for openness and the guidance of the Holy Spirit.
II. Reading of *Acts 2:42-47* and *Galatians 5:22*.
III. Period of silent reflection.
IV. Sharing.
- In what ways do we specifically need to improve our faithfulness to the apostles' instruction?
- How can we continue our learning process?
- In what ways do we specifically need to improve our faithfulness to this community and to the larger communities to which we belong?
- How can we make our love evident?
- What can we do to build the kingdom of God in our parish?
- In what ways do we specifically need to improve our faithfulness to the breaking of the bread?
- In what ways do we need to improve our faithfulness to prayer?
- Which of the following do I experience least in this community — Love — Joy — Peace — Patient Endurance — Kindess — Generosity — Faith — Gentleness — Self-Control?
- Which of the virtues must I develop personally?
V. Summary of decisions that have been made.
VI. Prayer service for forgiveness and healing.

Rearrange this format or make up your own. Determine how regularly you will hold such an evaluation, e.g., once every six months or once a year.

Prayer

Read *Luke 15:11-24*
Leader:
God loves us and eagerly waits for us to return to him. He does not wait for self-accusation and pleas for forgiveness, but rather runs to greet us at our first turning back. He covers us with loving words and gestures. Is our attitude towards those

who are ungrateful to us or hurt us the same as God's attitude towards us — eager to forgive, embrace, and express love?

Quiet reflection — 5 minutes

Leader: For our sins against love,
All: Father, forgive us as we forgive others.
Leader: For our sins against joy,
All: Father, forgive us as we forgive others.
Leader: For our sins against peace,
All: Father, forgive us as we forgive others.
Leader: For our sins against patience,
All: Father, forgive us as we forgive others.
Leader: For our sins against kindness,
All: Father, forgive us as we forgive others.
Leader: For our sins against goodness,
All: Father, forgive us as we forgive others.
Leader: For our sins against faithfulness,
All: Father, forgive us as we forgive others.
Leader: For our sins against self-control,
All: Father, forgive us as we forgive others.
Leader: Confident of our Father's forgiveness let us show each other a sign of love and forgiveness.

Join hands and sing, *Peace is Flowing Like a River* (from the album/cassette *I Will Never Forget You My People* by Carey Landry or listen to the song, *Sing to the Mountain* (from the album/cassette *Earthen Vessels* by the St. Louis Jesuits).

Faith in Action

Discuss the action which you had taken to alleviate some of the pain which people experience. Share the ways in which the people you serve are changing your lives.

Assignment

Faith in Action
Choose another need of which you are aware or contact your social concerns chairperson to identify an area of need.
Our Father: See suggested format.

Love, The Law
of Community

Opening Prayer

See suggested format.

Reflection

"The command I give you is this, that you love one another." *(John 15:17)*. Jesus makes his will for our community clear when he gives us the one law of love. The love he requires of us is a love to be seen openly by others. "This is how all will know you for my disciples: your love for one another." *(John 13:35)*. This love is not to be limited to the Christian community, but is to touch and change the world in very real ways. Our concern for others will be the source of our final judgment. *Read Matthew 25:31-46*.

One question remains, how do we know if our love is real? What are the qualities of true Christian love? St. Paul gives us a beautiful discourse to help us reflect on that question. In this reflection on the attributes of love, think about how your behavior has changed in each of these areas since you began meeting together as a community. Have you grown in your relationship to one another in this sharing group, with your family, with co-workers, with friends, with people in your parish and neighborhood, with the people with whom you are working to make this earth a love-filled global village?

Our love must be expressed as service. We are called to continue the mission of Jesus in the world. *Read Luke 4:14-21*. We are the instruments which God uses in this age to "bring glad tidings to the poor...liberty to the captives...recovery of sight to the blind...release to prisoners." We are the ones through whom God pours out his healing, his gentleness, his peace, his love.

Read the following message aloud. *I Corinthians 13:4-7*

Love is patient;
Love is kind,
Love is not jealous,
It does not put on airs,
It is not snobbish.
Love is never rude,
It is not self-seeking,

It is not prone to anger;
neither does *it* brood over injuries.
Love does not rejoice in what is wrong, but rejoices with
    the truth.
There is no limit to *love's* forbearance,
to *its* trust,
its hope,
its power to endure.

Reread the passage, placing the words *This Community*
everywhere that the word *Love* or *It* appears in the original.
Some quiet time should follow with everyone writing down
some examples which demonstrate how this community
exhibits the qualities of love. After about ten minutes everyone
could share his or her responses, and also talk about ways
that this community could improve its expressions of love
within the community and to all those outside this
sharing group.

A question now faces us. How would you like to develop
our small Christian community?

Share your thoughts regarding an on-going process of
growth for your community. Set aside time to evaluate
materials which are available for your use.

Prayer

Quiet reflection — 3 to 5 minutes

Leader: For calling us together to be a community of love,
All: We thank you, Father.
Leader: For the kindness we have experienced,
All: We thank you, Father.
Leader: For the joy we have shared,
All: We thank you, Father.
Leader: For the forbearance we have experienced,
All: We thank you, Father.
Leader: For the hope we have shared,
All: We thank you, Father.
Leader: For the endurance we have experienced,
All: We thank you, Father.
Leader: For the faith we have shared,
All: We thank you, Father.
Leader:*For
All: We thank you, Father.

*Each person take a turn naming the person on his/her left.
  All respond to each name, "We thank you, Father."

Play the song, *We Thank You, Father* (from the album/cassette *Locusts and Wild Honey* by The Weston Priory).

Faith in Action

Continue to coordinate your services with the Social Concerns Committee of your parish council.

Our Father: See suggested format.

"SMALL GROUP SHARING" MATERIALS

The Experience of Lent with the Risen Christ
by Sister Catherine Nerney, S.S.J.
This six-week reflection series invites us to repent and believe the Good News.
$1.50 net

Share Your Bread
by Sister Joan Jungerman, S.S.N.D.
A prayerful, reflective seven-part Lenten booklet designed to help us take stock, and to look for areas in which we must change. $1.50 net

Building Christian Community
by Catherine Martin
This program is designed for use by all who are willing to make serious efforts to build a Christian community in which loving persons pray and reflect, learn and serve together. $1.50 net

Spiritual Growth
by Sister Joan Jungerman, S.S.N.D.
This twelve-session booklet, based on St. John's Gospel, calls participants to reflection, prayer, discussion and outreach. $1.50 net

"SMALL GROUP SHARING" RESOURCE BOOKS

Prayers for the Seasons
by Lois Kikkert, O.P.
A book of prayer experiences designed for use within the entire parish. Its purpose is to provide a prayerful atmosphere form which any business meeting can flow.
$1.75 net

Building for Justice: A Guide for Social Concerns Committees
ed. John Bins
A guidebook filled with practical helps and suggestions for parish social concerns groups as they start and as they grow. $1.75 net

Moving Towards Small Christian Communities, An On-Going Model of Parish Life
by Msgr. Thomas A. Kleissler, Catherine Martin, and Rev. Joseph T. Slinger
A booklet designed to show how small communities can be an integral part of parish life. $1.75 net

Thy Kingdom Come
by Mary Elizabeth Clark, S.S.J.
A collection of twenty-four prayer sessions designed to provide a spiritual foundation for social concerns groups. $1.75 net

"SMALL GROUP SHARING" PRAYER LEAFLETS
(for your parishioners during Lent)

Change and Believe!
by Rev. Kenneth J. St. Amand
A collection of thoughts for each day of Lent for those Christians interested in responding to the invitation of Christ during this season of grace.
50 leaflets for $10.00 net

Journey with Paul
by Rev. John J. Gilchrist
Brief Scriptural reflections and comments contained in a pocket-size booklet of daily Lenten meditations. 50 leaflets for $10.00 net